RECIPES REMEMBERED

These are the collected recipes and memories of the

_____

FAMILY

COMPILED BY

_____

BEGUN ON

_____

FAMILY
PHOTOGRAPH

All human history attests
That happiness for man—the hungry sinner!
Since Eve ate apples, much depends on dinner.
—Lord Byron

RECIPES REMEMBERED

Conceived and Written by
MARCIA ADAMS

Illustrated by
DEB MORES

Gramercy Books
New York

This 2000 edition is published by Gramercy Books™,
an imprint of Random House Value Publishing, Inc.,
280 Park Avenue, New York, NY 10017, by arrangement with Clarkson N. Potter, Inc.,
a member of the Crown Publishing Group of Random House, Inc.

Gramercy Books™ and design are trademarks of
Random House Value Publishing, Inc.

Printed in Singapore

Random House
New York • Toronto • London • Sydney • Auckland
http://www.randomhouse.com/

Design by Nancy Kenmore

A catalog record for this title is available from the Library of Congress

ISBN: 0-517-20896-2

9 8 7 6 5 4 3 2

Contents

INTRODUCTION

One summer, many years ago, my mother was recuperating from surgery and came to stay with me for nearly a month. As always, whenever we were together, there was a great deal of talk about food and recipes, with lots of reminiscing. I got out my recipe file, which was then still on cards—this was long before word pro-cessors—to discuss the fine points of some of the family rec-ipes she'd given me earlier. We discovered there seemed to be discrepancies, and it occurred to us both that this was the time to redo the recipes and "get them down right" once and for all.

Anyone who can read can cook.
— Marcia Adams

So for the rest of her convalescing visit with me, I cooked and washed dishes, while she instructed and sampled, and we both agreed it was the most fun we had had in ages. Looking back now, I realize what a privilege it was to have had that time with her to record not only the recipes, but the memories she associated with them.

Anyone who has read my cookbooks or watched my television series knows of my passion for "attic receipts." In every interview I give, I plead for families to record their recipes, past and present—the ones their grandmothers made, the ones their mothers didn't write down, and the ones the daughters now want to pass onto *their* families. These heirloom recipes are part of your family history and its traditions. Equally important are your favorite recipes today, and how you are keeping traditions from the past alive and fostering new ones—the little details that make your family unique and special. When it has been filled with your unique food history and the recipes that go along with it, this book can be one of the most precious gifts you give to your family.

I've included a handful of my own culinary heirlooms. Some of these recipes have appeared in my earlier cookbooks, and by request, many have been shared with my sons and my nieces. Some are always served at family dinners and holidays. Those recipes, scribbled down on drowsy July afternoons at my kitchen table, over lemonade and cookies, are a link with my family—my tribe, if you please. Through those recipes, we as a collective family reinforce our ties to one another.

How I Learned to Cook

My salad days when I was green in judgment . . .
—Cleopatra

People learn to cook in many ways: from a parent, from a grandparent, in a home economics class, or even from cookbooks or cooking classes. I learned to cook from _____
_____
_____

Some of the earliest dishes I prepared were:_____
_____
_____

These are some of my favorite first recipes.

RECIPE_____

INGREDIENTS_____   _____

_____   _____

_____   _____

_____   _____

_____   _____

_____   _____

INSTRUCTIONS_____

_____

_____

_____

_____

_____

SERVES_____   SOURCE_____

RECIPE_____

INGREDIENTS_____   _____

_____   _____

_____   _____

_____   _____

_____   _____

INSTRUCTIONS_____

_____

_____

_____

_____

_____

SERVES_____   SOURCE_____

RECIPE_____

INGREDIENTS_____   _____

_____   _____

_____   _____

_____   _____

_____   _____

INSTRUCTIONS_____

_____

_____

_____

_____

_____

SERVES_____   SOURCE_____

RECIPE_____

INGREDIENTS_____   _____

_____   _____

_____   _____

_____   _____

_____   _____

INSTRUCTIONS_____

_____

_____

_____

_____

_____

SERVES_____ SOURCE_____

The very first meal I ever prepared all by myself was _____

_____

I made it for _____

_____

It was _____ !!

As I refined my cooking skills, I developed several specialties that I enjoyed cooking for family and friends. I was often asked to make _____

_____

_____

I was proudest of the time I cooked _____

_____

My worst cooking disaster was _____

_____

_____

_____

MY MOTHER'S RECIPES

Cuisine is when things taste like themselves.
—*Curnonsky*

My mother's cooking was most influenced by _____
_____

She was best known for _____
_____

Here are some of her favorite recipes.

RECIPE _____
INGREDIENTS _____   _____
_____   _____
_____   _____
_____   _____
_____   _____
_____   _____

INSTRUCTIONS _____
_____
_____
_____
_____
_____
_____

SERVES _____

RECIPE

INGREDIENTS

INSTRUCTIONS

SERVES

RECIPE

INGREDIENTS

INSTRUCTIONS

SERVES

RECIPE_____

INGREDIENTS_____ | _____

_____ | _____

_____ | _____

_____ | _____

_____ | _____

INSTRUCTIONS_____

_____

_____

_____

_____

_____

SERVES_____

RECIPE_____

INGREDIENTS_____ | _____

_____ | _____

_____ | _____

_____ | _____

_____ | _____

INSTRUCTIONS_____

_____

_____

_____

_____

_____

SERVES_____

I Remember . . .
VERY COMFORTING CHICKEN SOUP

◆

Well, don't we all remember chicken soup? However, it's rather hard to achieve that hearty chicken flavor because now our supermarket chickens are just young things. I ask you, when did you last hear a rooster crow, or see an old hen scratching in a yard? Those old birds and their bones gave the soup of our recollections its flavor. To re-create it today, I suggest starting with a base of chicken broth rather than water and sautéing some of the vegetables first. Do chop the vegetables by hand, not in a food processor. This is quite a thick soup, a one-dish meal actually, with a bit of barley and noodles and lots of chicken meat, and not many fat grams. Leftovers freeze very well indeed.

2 pounds chicken breasts, skinned,
   bone in
2 pounds chicken thighs, skinned,
   bone in
6 cans (15 ounces each) low-fat chicken
   broth
1 bay leaf
8 whole cloves
1 tablespoon vegetable oil
2 cups chopped celery
1 cup chopped onion
1 small green bell pepper, chopped
2 cups thin egg noodles
$^1/_2$ cup quick-cooking barley
1 cup coarsely grated carrot (use food
   processor, if you prefer)
1 cup fresh or frozen green peas
$^1/_2$ cup chopped fresh parsley
1 teaspoon ground poultry seasoning
1 teaspoon dried thyme
Salt and pepper to taste

Place the chicken pieces in a large soup pot and cover with the broth. Add the bay leaf and cloves (you can place these in a bit of cheesecloth and tie it closed, or pick them out individually later), cover, and bring to a boil. Immediately lower the heat and simmer for 20 minutes or until the chicken is tender. Skim off the foam with a large spoon and discard.

Meanwhile, in a sauté pan, heat the oil over low heat. Add the celery, onion, and bell pepper and sauté slowly, stirring often, until the vegetables turn golden, about 20 minutes.

When the chicken is tender, with tongs remove it from the broth to a flat dish and allow the chicken to cool slightly. Remove the chicken from the bones in large, bite-size pieces; set aside. Remove the bay leaf and cloves from the broth and discard them.

Return the broth to a broil and gradually add the noodles and barley; cover and simmer for 10 minutes. Add the rest of the ingredients, including the reserved chicken, and simmer 10 minutes longer, or until the barley and vegetables are tender. Serve immediately.

MAKES 4 QUARTS

RECIPE_____

INGREDIENTS_____   _____

_____   _____

_____   _____

_____   _____

_____   _____

_____   _____

INSTRUCTIONS_____

_____

_____

_____

_____

_____

SERVES_____

RECIPE_____

INGREDIENTS_____   _____

_____   _____

_____   _____

_____   _____

_____   _____

INSTRUCTIONS_____

_____

_____

_____

_____

SERVES_____

My Father's Favorite Foods

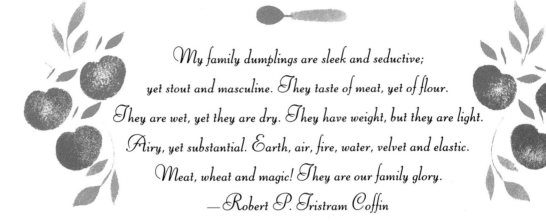

My family dumplings are sleek and seductive;
yet stout and masculine. They taste of meat, yet of flour.
They are wet, yet they are dry. They have weight, but they are light.
Airy, yet substantial. Earth, air, fire, water, velvet and elastic.
Meat, wheat and magic! They are our family glory.
—Robert P. Tristram Coffin

Here are the recipes my father liked most.

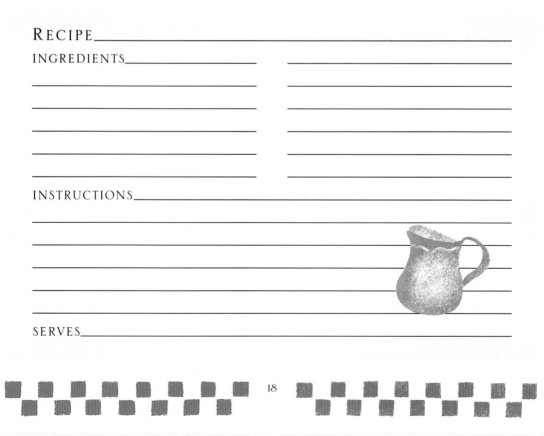

RECIPE_____

INGREDIENTS_____   _____

_____   _____

_____   _____

_____   _____

_____   _____

_____

INSTRUCTIONS_____

_____

_____

_____

_____

_____

SERVES_____

RECIPE_____

INGREDIENTS_____

_____   _____

_____   _____

_____   _____

_____   _____

_____   _____

INSTRUCTIONS_____

_____

_____

_____

_____

_____

SERVES_____

I Remember . . .

FLUFFY DUMPLINGS

———◆———

My mother, with her Irish and Pennsylvania Dutch background, was a very good baker. Among the delicacies she made, my favorite was her dumplings, which she would drop on top of soups, chicken fricassee, beef stew, or stewed tomatoes, or even on rhubarb sauce or cooked blueberries. These are fluffy and finely grained dumplings; you can adapt them to different uses by varying the spices or herbs.

1 cup all-purpose flour
1 1/2 teaspoons baking powder
1/2 teaspoon salt
1 egg
1 tablespoon vegetable oil

6 tablespoons milk
2 tablespoons finely minced fresh herbs, such as dill, parsley, or marjoram, OR 1/2 teaspoon dried, OR 1/2 teaspoon ground spice, such as cinnamon or nutmeg

In a medium bowl, whisk together the flour, baking powder, and salt. In a small bowl, beat the egg thoroughly, then blend in the oil, milk, and seasonings. Pour the milk mixture over the dry ingredients and blend just until combined; don't overmix. Drop the batter by tablespoons on top of the simmering mixture of your choice (stew, broth, or fruit). Cover tightly and cook over medium-low heat for 20 minutes *without* lifting the lid. Serve the dumplings in bowls.

SERVES 4 TO 6

SPECIALTIES FROM MY GRANDPARENTS

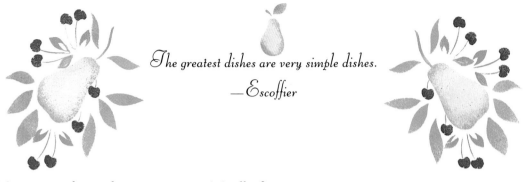

The greatest dishes are very simple dishes.
—Escoffier

My maternal grandparents were originally from _____
and the family's cooking was influenced most by _____
_____

Whenever we went to their house, we always were served _____
_____

Here are some of the family recipes that I loved best.

RECIPE _____
INGREDIENTS _____   _____
_____   _____
_____   _____
_____   _____
_____   _____

INSTRUCTIONS _____
_____
_____
_____
_____

SERVES _____

RECIPE

INGREDIENTS

INSTRUCTIONS

SERVES

RECIPE

INGREDIENTS

INSTRUCTIONS

SERVES

RECIPE_____

INGREDIENTS_____ _____

_____ _____

_____ _____

_____ _____

_____ _____

_____ _____

INSTRUCTIONS_____

_____

_____

_____

_____

_____

SERVES_____

RECIPE_____

INGREDIENTS_____ _____

_____ _____

_____ _____

_____ _____

_____ _____

INSTRUCTIONS_____

_____

_____

_____

_____

_____

SERVES_____

I Remember . . .

GOLDEN MACE CAKE WITH LEMON SAUCE

---◆---

This was a favorite of my Grandmother Manahan. It is easy to make and has a nice texture. She would sometimes frost the cake with chocolate, penuche, or seven-minute frosting, but she most often served it with a tart hot lemon sauce. This sauce is also good over gingerbread or steamed puddings, and it can be reheated in the microwave.

CAKE
1 1/4 cups all-purpose flour
1 cup sugar
1 1/2 teaspoons baking powder
1/2 teaspoon salt
1/4 teaspoon, rounded, ground mace
1/3 cup butter, at room temperature
3/4 cup milk, at room temperature
1 egg, at room temperature
2 teaspoons vanilla extract

SAUCE
2 large eggs, well beaten
2 cups sugar
1 cup (2 sticks) butter
1/2 cup water
1/3 cup fresh lemon juice
2 teaspoons grated lemon zest
1/2 teaspoon almond extract

To make the cake, preheat the oven to 350° F. Grease and flour a 9-inch square pan. Measure the flour, sugar, baking powder, salt, and mace into the bowl of an electric mixer; blend briefly. Add the butter, milk, egg, and vanilla and blend for 30 seconds on low speed, scraping the bowl constantly. Turn the mixer speed to high and beat 3 minutes longer, scraping the bowl occasionally. Pour into the prepared pan. Bake for 35 to 40 minutes, or until the cake is golden brown and begins to shrink away from the sides of the pan. Cool in the pan and cut into squares.

To make the sauce, combine all of the ingredients in a medium saucepan. Bring to a boil over medium heat, and cook, whisking now and then, for about 8 minutes. Ladle over each serving.

MAKES 9 TO 12 SERVINGS

My paternal grandparents were originally from _____
and the family's cooking was most influenced by _____
_____

Whenever we went to their house, we always were served_____
_____

On the next pages are some of the family recipes that I remember best.

RECIPE_____

INGREDIENTS_____   _____

_____   _____

_____   _____

_____   _____

_____   _____

INSTRUCTIONS_____

_____

_____

_____

_____

_____

SERVES_____

RECIPE_____

INGREDIENTS_____   _____

_____   _____

_____   _____

_____   _____

_____   _____

INSTRUCTIONS_____

_____

_____

_____

_____

_____

SERVES_____

RECIPE_____

INGREDIENTS_____   _____

_____   _____

_____   _____

_____   _____

_____

INSTRUCTIONS_____

_____

_____

_____

_____

SERVES_____

I Remember . . .

APPLE CHUTNEY

———◆———

My paternal grandmother, Ella Lucas Grabill, en-
tertained with great style and always served her
food on the most attractive dishes. Also a fine gar-
dener, she took special pride in her orchard and
raised many varieties of apples. She made this
chutney every fall, and I still remember the spicy
fragrance of her kitchen as it simmered on the
back of her black iron wood-burning stove.

2 pounds cooking apples, peeled, cored,
and coarsely chopped
2 pounds ripe tomatoes, peeled, cored,
and coarsely chopped
2 cups coarsely chopped onions
1 pound seedless raisins

2 pounds brown sugar
1 quart cider vinegar
2 tablespoons mustard seed
1 tablespoon curry powder
2 teaspoons salt
1 teaspoon ground allspice
1 teaspoon ground coriander
1 teaspoon ground cumin
1 teaspoon ground ginger
$^1/_2$ teaspoon ground cloves

In a large stockpot, combine all of the ingredients. Bring the mixture to a boil, lower the heat,
and simmer uncovered for $1^1/_2$ to 2 hours, or
until the chutney is thick but is still a bit runny.

Ladle into sterilized 1-pint jars, leaving a
$^1/_4$-inch headspace; adjust the lids and rings and
process for 10 minutes, or freeze.

MAKES 4 PINTS

WEDDING MEMORIES

Everything happens at parties.
—*Jane Austen*

Our wedding took place at _____

The meal served was _____

The wedding cake was _____

These are some of the foods that were served at the prenuptial parties and at the wedding reception.

RECIPE_____

INGREDIENTS_____   _____

_____   _____

_____   _____

_____   _____

_____   _____

_____   _____

INSTRUCTIONS_____

_____

_____

_____

_____

_____

SERVES_____   SOURCE_____

RECIPE_____

INGREDIENTS_____ _____

_____ _____

_____ _____

_____ _____

_____

INSTRUCTIONS_____

_____

_____

_____

_____

_____

SERVES_____ SOURCE_____

RECIPE_____

INGREDIENTS_____ _____

_____ _____

_____ _____

_____ _____

_____ _____

INSTRUCTIONS_____

_____

_____

_____

_____

_____

SERVES_____ SOURCE_____

I Remember . . .
SHRIMP TRUFFLES

———◆———

I would love to have known what was served at my parents wedding but, alas, my mother no longer remembered when I asked her. When Dick and I married it was a second wedding for both of us, we each had a son, and it was a small family affair. The reception was held at our house-to-be. There was a wedding cake with not only a bride and groom on top, but two small boys as well. With this, I served champagne, a nonalcoholic fruit punch for the children, and assorted hors d'oeuvres, including this recipe I'd clipped from our local paper. I made everything myself. And, oh yes, I carried creamy white gardenias.

1 package (8 ounces) cream cheese, softened
1 cup chopped, cooked shrimp, chilled
2 teaspoons finely minced parsley
1 1/2 teaspoons Dijon mustard
1 teaspoon finely minced onion
1 teaspoon lemon juice
2 drops hot red pepper sauce
Salt and pepper to taste
1 1/2 cups finely chopped toasted pecans

In a medium bowl, combine all of the ingredients except the nuts. Refrigerate overnight. Place the nuts in a shallow dish, then form the cheese mixture into 1-inch balls. Roll the balls in the nuts and refrigerate until serving time.

MAKES 3 1/2 DOZEN HORS D'OEUVRES

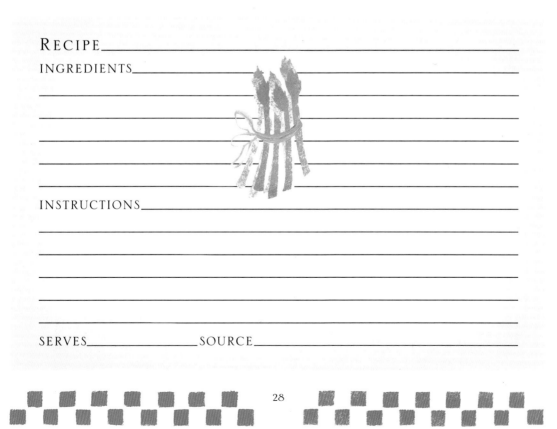

RECIPE_____

INGREDIENTS_____

_____

_____

_____

_____

_____

INSTRUCTIONS_____

_____

_____

_____

_____

_____

SERVES_____ SOURCE_____

HOLIDAY RECIPES

The proof of the pudding

is in the eating.

—Cervantes, Don Quixote

Of all the holidays, our family most enjoyed_____

One food you could always find on our holiday table was_____

Here are some holiday favorites.

Remembered Recipes for Thanksgiving

RECIPE_____

INGREDIENTS_____ _____

_____ _____

_____ _____

_____ _____

_____ _____

_____ _____

INSTRUCTIONS_____

_____

_____

_____

_____

_____

_____

SERVES_____ SOURCE_____

RECIPE_____

INGREDIENTS_____   _____

_____   _____

_____   _____

_____   _____

_____   _____

INSTRUCTIONS_____

_____

_____

_____

_____

_____

SERVES_____ SOURCE_____

I Remember . . .

EASY PIE PASTRY

—◆—

Of all our favorite family desserts, pie receives the highest marks. If it is in a crust, it will be relished. This recipe came to me from "The Settlers," a group of Fort Wayne women who meet regularly to teach old American crafts and foodways. A flavorful golden pastry, made with an electric mixer, it handles beautifully and comes out perfect every time.

> *4 cups all-purpose flour*
> *1 tablespoon sugar*
> *2 teaspoons salt*
> *$1^3/_4$ cups butter-flavored solid vegetable shortening*

> *1 large egg*
> *1 tablespoon cider vinegar*
> *$^1/_2$ cup water*

Combine the flour, sugar, salt, and shortening in a large bowl of an electric mixer and blend on medium speed until it has the texture of coarse crumbs. In a small bowl, beat the egg, vinegar, and water. Drizzle over the flour mixture and mix thoroughly until it forms a soft dough. Shape the dough into a patty, wrap in plastic wrap, and place in the freezer for 45 minutes, or refrigerate overnight. Form the dough into a long roll, divide into fourths, wrap each portion, and chill or freeze. Remove the dough from the refrigerator 30 minutes in advance of rolling.

MAKES ENOUGH PASTRY FOR TWO
DOUBLE CRUST PIES

RECIPE

INGREDIENTS

INSTRUCTIONS

SERVES_____ SOURCE_____

RECIPE

INGREDIENTS

INSTRUCTIONS

SERVES_____ SOURCE_____

RECIPE_____

INGREDIENTS_____

_____

_____

_____

_____

_____

INSTRUCTIONS_____

_____

_____

_____

_____

_____

SERVES_____ SOURCE_____

RECIPE_____

INGREDIENTS_____   _____

_____   _____

_____   _____

_____   _____

_____   _____

INSTRUCTIONS_____

_____

_____

_____

_____

_____

SERVES_____ SOURCE_____

RECIPE_____

INGREDIENTS_____   _____

_____   _____

_____   _____

_____   _____

_____   _____

INSTRUCTIONS_____

_____

_____

_____

_____

SERVES_____ SOURCE_____

RECIPE_____

INGREDIENTS_____   _____

_____   _____

_____   _____

_____   _____

_____   _____

INSTRUCTIONS_____

_____

_____

_____

_____

SERVES_____ SOURCE_____

RECIPE_____

INGREDIENTS_____   _____

_____   _____

_____   _____

_____   _____

_____   _____

INSTRUCTIONS_____

_____

_____

_____

_____

_____

SERVES_____   SOURCE_____

RECIPE_____

INGREDIENTS_____   _____

_____   _____

_____   _____

_____   _____

_____   _____

INSTRUCTIONS_____

_____

_____

_____

_____

_____

SERVES_____   SOURCE_____

RECIPE_____

INGREDIENTS_____   _____

_____   _____

_____   _____

_____   _____

_____   _____

INSTRUCTIONS_____

_____

_____

_____

_____

_____

SERVES_____   SOURCE_____

RECIPE_____

INGREDIENTS_____

_____

_____

_____

_____

_____

INSTRUCTIONS_____

_____

_____

_____

_____

SERVES_____   SOURCE_____

FAMILY GATHERINGS

*Strange to see
how a good dinner and feasting
reconciles everybody.*
—Samuel Pepys

The family usually gathered at _____

The group included _____

_____

These are some of the family specialties I remember most vividly.

RECIPE _____

INGREDIENTS _____ _____

_____ _____

_____ _____

_____ _____

_____ _____

INSTRUCTIONS _____

_____

_____

_____

_____

SERVES _____ SOURCE _____

OCCASION WHEN IT WAS PREPARED _____

RECIPE_____

INGREDIENTS_____   _____

_____   _____

_____   _____

_____   _____

_____   _____

INSTRUCTIONS_____

_____

_____

_____

_____

SERVES_____   SOURCE_____

OCCASION WHEN IT WAS PREPARED_____

RECIPE_____

INGREDIENTS_____   _____

_____

_____

_____

_____

_____

INSTRUCTIONS_____

_____

_____

_____

_____

SERVES_____   SOURCE_____

OCCASION WHEN IT WAS PREPARED_____

I Remember . . .
AUNT ONIE'S GINGERBREAD MUFFINS WITH CURRANTS

—◆—

My Aunt Onie was the family eccentric; she always brought her own drinking water to our family reunions. Today that wouldn't be considered too unusual, but then it was positively weird. Because she was a fine cook, however, we generally overlooked the fact that she was, well, a little peculiar. I suspect every family has one such relative. Staying at her house was a pleasure, for we could count on wonderful cookies, pies, and cakes, and for breakfast, delicate gingerbread muffins that she made from a batter stored in a crock in the cool milk house.

The original recipe was made with lard, but I have substituted vegetable shortening with excellent results. Prepare the batter at least a day in advance. The recipe yields two dozen muffins, but I usually bake just a few at a time because the batter keeps so well.

> 1 teaspoon baking soda
> 1 teaspoon vanilla extract
> $^1/_2$ cup buttermilk
> $^3/_4$ cup solid vegetable shortening
> $^1/_2$ cup granulated sugar
> $^1/_2$ cup light brown sugar, packed
> 2 large eggs
> $^1/_2$ cup molasses or dark corn syrup

> 2 cups all-purpose flour
> $^1/_2$ teaspoon salt
> 2 teaspoons ground ginger
> $^1/_2$ teaspoon ground cinnamon
> $^1/_2$ teaspoon ground nutmeg
> $^1/_2$ teaspoon ground allspice
> $^1/_2$ teaspoon ground cloves
> $^1/_4$ teaspoon ground black pepper
> $^1/_4$ cup finely chopped pecans or black walnuts
> $^1/_4$ cup dried currants

In a small mixing bowl, whisk together the soda, vanilla, and buttermilk; set aside and allow to foam. In a large bowl of an electric mixer, beat the shortening for a few seconds; gradually add the sugars and beat for 5 minutes. Add the eggs one at a time and blend well. Beat in the molasses.

In a large bowl whisk together the flour, salt, and spices. Add to the creamed mixture alternately with the buttermilk, beginning and ending with the flour mixture. Blend well, then stir in the nuts and currants. Transfer the batter to a plastic container, cover tightly, and refrigerate overnight or up to two weeks.

Preheat the oven to 325° F. Line muffin tins with paper liners and spoon the batter into the cups, filling about three-fourths full. Bake for 20 to 25 minutes, or until the muffins are firm on top when touched with your fingertip. Serve hot with butter.

MAKES 24 MUFFINS

The Supper Table

I hate people who are not serious about their meals.
—Oscar Wilde

Whether it was a carry-in pizza or an elaborate banquet, we always tried to gather each day for the evening meal. We usually ate at _____
Each family member had a chore:_____
_____

Here is what we liked best.

RECIPE_____
INGREDIENTS_____   _____
_____   _____
_____   _____
_____   _____
_____   _____
_____   _____

INSTRUCTIONS_____
_____
_____
_____
_____
_____

SERVES_____   SOURCE_____

RECIPE_____

INGREDIENTS_____   _____

_____   _____

_____   _____

_____   _____

_____   _____

_____

INSTRUCTIONS_____

_____

_____

_____

_____

_____

_____

SERVES_____SOURCE_____

RECIPE_____

INGREDIENTS_____   _____

_____   _____

_____   _____

_____   _____

_____   _____

_____

INSTRUCTIONS_____

_____

_____

_____

_____

_____

_____

SERVES_____SOURCE_____

I Remember . . .

MOIST AND FLAVORFUL
MEAT LOAF

———◆———

My mother experimented with this recipe, adding various things until she finally had it "right"—right meaning that our whole family was enthusiastic about this rather economical main dish.

2 eggs, lightly beaten
$^1/_2$ cup chopped celery
$^1/_2$ cup chopped onion
$^1/_2$ cup chopped parsley
$^1/_4$ cup chopped green bell pepper
2 tablespoons prepared horseradish
1 teaspoon ground mustard
1 teaspoon salt

$^1/_2$ teaspoon pepper
2 pounds ground round beef
1 pound ground pork loin
$1^1/_2$ cups fresh bread crumbs
1 can (6 ounces) vegetable cocktail
$^1/_2$ to $^3/_4$ cup chili sauce

Preheat the oven to 350° F. In a large bowl, combine the eggs, celery, onion, parsley, bell pepper, horseradish, mustard, salt, and pepper. Crumble in the ground meats, then add the bread crumbs and vegetable cocktail. Mix lightly, using your hands if necessary. Transfer the mixture to a greased 13 X 9-inch flat pan and pat it into an 11 X 6-inch loaf. Top with the chili sauce.

Bake the loaf uncovered for 1 hour. Remove the loaf from the oven and allow to stand loosely covered with foil for 10 minutes before cutting.

SERVES 10 TO 12

RECIPE

INGREDIENTS

INSTRUCTIONS

SERVES_____ SOURCE

CHILDREN'S FAVORITES AND SPECIAL REQUESTS

There is no love sincerer
than the love of food.
—George Bernard Shaw

My children's all-time favorite foods were: _____
_____
_____

Below are the special family dishes we made to celebrate returning home from camp, when pampering was needed, or to honor a promotion or good grades.

RECIPE_____

INGREDIENTS_____   _____
_____   _____
_____   _____
_____   _____
_____   _____

INSTRUCTIONS_____
_____
_____
_____
_____

SERVES_____ SOURCE_____
MADE FOR_____

RECIPE_____

INGREDIENTS_____   _____

_____   _____

_____   _____

_____   _____

_____   _____

_____

INSTRUCTIONS_____

_____

_____

_____

_____

SERVES_____   SOURCE_____

MADE FOR_____

RECIPE_____

INGREDIENTS_____   _____

_____   _____

_____   _____

_____   _____

_____   _____

_____

INSTRUCTIONS_____

_____

_____

_____

_____

SERVES_____   SOURCE_____

MADE FOR_____

RECIPE_____

INGREDIENTS_____   _____

_____   _____

_____   _____

_____   _____

_____   _____

INSTRUCTIONS_____

_____

_____

_____

_____

_____

SERVES_____ SOURCE_____

MADE FOR_____

I Remember . . .

LARRY'S LEMON CREAM PIE

——◆——

My stepson, Larry, and I really got acquainted by working together in the kitchen. To my surprise he loved baking and could knead brioche like a pro. I also discovered his favorite dessert was lemon pie, so whenever he was the focus of a special meal, I always made this tart creamy pie.

Rounded $^1/_4$ cup of cornstarch

$^1/_2$ cup cold water

4 large egg yolks

2 cups sugar

Grated zest and juice of 2 lemons

$^1/_8$ teaspoon salt

2 cups boiling water

1 baked 9-inch pastry shell

$^1/_2$ cup heavy cream, whipped and sweetened

2 to 3 tablespoons finely chopped pecans

In a small bowl, blend the cornstarch and water until smooth. In the top of a double boiler, beat the egg yolks thoroughly. Add the sugar, lemon zest and juice, and salt; combine well. Pour in the cornstarch mixture and blend. Add the boiling water and whisk until smooth. Cook the mixture over hot water, stirring frequently with a rubber spatula, until the mixture thickens, about 20 to 30 minutes. Chill the custard thoroughly. Transfer the chilled custard to the baked pie shell. Top with the sweetened whipped cream and sprinkle with the nuts. Refrigerate until ready to serve.

MAKES 6 TO 8 SERVINGS

RECIPE_____

INGREDIENTS_____ _____

_____ _____

_____ _____

_____ _____

_____ _____

_____ _____

INSTRUCTIONS_____

_____

_____

_____

_____

SERVES_____SOURCE_____

MADE FOR_____

RECIPE_____

INGREDIENTS_____ _____

_____ _____

_____ _____

_____ _____

_____ _____

_____ _____

INSTRUCTIONS_____

_____

_____

_____

_____

SERVES_____SOURCE_____

MADE FOR_____

BIRTHDAY CELEBRATIONS

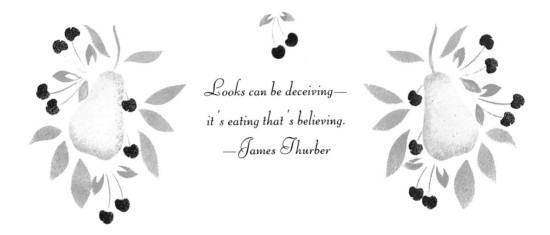

Looks can be deceiving—
it's eating that's believing.
—James Thurber

On birthdays, we made a special meal for the birthday child, complete with his or her favorite cake or dessert. Here is each family member's birthday indulgence.

RECIPE_____

INGREDIENTS_____   _____

_____   _____

_____   _____

_____   _____

_____   _____

_____   _____

INSTRUCTIONS_____

_____

_____

_____

_____

SERVES_____ SOURCE_____

MADE FOR_____

RECIPE_____

INGREDIENTS_____   _____

_____   _____

_____   _____

_____   _____

_____   _____

INSTRUCTIONS_____

_____

_____

_____

_____

SERVES_____SOURCE_____

MADE FOR_____

RECIPE_____

INGREDIENTS_____   _____

_____   _____

_____   _____

_____   _____

_____   _____

INSTRUCTIONS_____

_____

_____

_____

_____

SERVES_____SOURCE_____

MADE FOR_____

RECIPE_____

INGREDIENTS_____ _____

_____ _____

_____ _____

_____ _____

_____ _____

_____

INSTRUCTIONS_____

_____

_____

_____

_____

_____

SERVES_____SOURCE_____

MADE FOR_____

RECIPE_____

INGREDIENTS_____ _____

_____ _____

_____ _____

_____ _____

_____ _____

_____ _____

INSTRUCTIONS_____

_____

_____

_____

_____

SERVES_____SOURCE_____

MADE FOR_____

SNACKS

Whenever we prepare snack foods for the whole family to enjoy, these are favorites.

RECIPE_____

INGREDIENTS_____   _____

_____   _____

_____   _____

_____   _____

_____   _____

_____   _____

INSTRUCTIONS_____

_____

_____

_____

_____

SERVES_____ SOURCE_____

RECIPE_____

INGREDIENTS_____   _____

_____

_____

_____   _____

_____   _____

INSTRUCTIONS_____

_____

_____

_____

_____

SERVES_____ SOURCE_____

PICNIC FOOD

*Nothing helps scenery
like ham and eggs.
— Mark Twain*

Some of the most memorable outings were:_____
_____
_____

These are some of the foods that I always like to take along on picnics.

RECIPE_____

INGREDIENTS_____   _____

_____   _____

_____   _____

_____   _____

_____   _____

_____   _____

INSTRUCTIONS_____

_____

_____

_____

_____

_____

SERVES_____SOURCE_____

RECIPE

INGREDIENTS

INSTRUCTIONS

SERVES_____ SOURCE_____

RECIPE

INGREDIENTS

INSTRUCTIONS

SERVES_____ SOURCE_____

READY FOR COMPANY

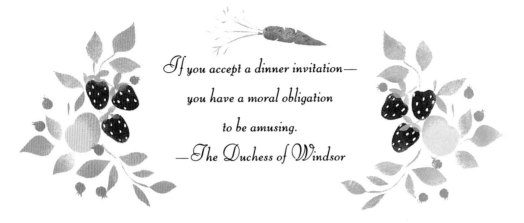

If you accept a dinner invitation—
you have a moral obligation
to be amusing.
—The Duchess of Windsor

My favorite way to entertain is_____

I am frequently asked to make_____

Here are some of my most successful recipes for entertaining.

RECIPE_____

INGREDIENTS_____   _____

_____   _____

_____   _____

_____   _____

_____   _____

INSTRUCTIONS_____

_____

_____

_____

_____

_____

SERVES_____   SOURCE_____

RECIPE_____

INGREDIENTS_____

_____

_____

_____

_____

_____

INSTRUCTIONS_____

_____

_____

_____

_____

_____

SERVES_____ SOURCE_____

RECIPE_____

INGREDIENTS_____   _____

_____   _____

_____   _____

_____   _____

_____   _____

INSTRUCTIONS_____

_____

_____

_____

_____

_____

SERVES_____ SOURCE_____

RECIPE_____

INGREDIENTS_____   _____

_____   _____

_____   _____

_____   _____

_____   _____

_____   _____

INSTRUCTIONS_____

_____

_____

_____

_____

_____

_____

SERVES_____   SOURCE_____

RECIPE_____

INGREDIENTS_____   _____

_____   _____

_____   _____

_____   _____

_____   _____

_____   _____

INSTRUCTIONS_____

_____

_____

_____

_____

_____

SERVES_____   SOURCE_____

RECIPE

INGREDIENTS

INSTRUCTIONS

SERVES_____ SOURCE_____

RECIPE

INGREDIENTS

INSTRUCTIONS

SERVES_____ SOURCE_____

FROM THE KITCHENS OF FRIENDS

*Many a one have been comforted
in their sorrow by seeing a good dish
come upon the table.*
— E. F. Gaskell

Through the years, friends have shared their very special favorite recipes with me. These are some of those I use most often.

RECIPE_____

INGREDIENTS_____   _____

_____   _____

_____   _____

_____   _____

_____   _____

_____   _____

INSTRUCTIONS_____

_____

_____

_____

_____

_____

SERVES_____   SOURCE_____

RECIPE_____

INGREDIENTS_____   _____

_____   _____

_____   _____

_____   _____

_____

INSTRUCTIONS_____

_____

_____

_____

_____

_____

SERVES_____ SOURCE_____

I Remember . . .

MRS. HEINY'S WHITE SAUCE

—◆—

This is a basic white or béchamel sauce. The sauce is still taught in all high-school home economics classes—or should be—because this is a recipe that cooks use over and over again. I look back and marvel at all the skills Mrs. Heiny, my home ec teacher, introduced to us. We learned to bake quick breads and yeast breads and to prepare an assortment of sauces, meat dishes, vegetables, butter cakes, and pies. Plus baby care. And her sewing classes were legendary; all her students won the blue and purple ribbons at the county 4-H fair.

¹/₄ cup butter
¹/₄ cup all-purpose flour
2 cups milk
¹/₈ teaspoon nutmeg
Salt and pepper to taste

In a medium saucepan, melt the butter over moderate heat; do not allow it to brown. Add the flour all at once, whisking and cooking until the mixture bubbles up in the center of the pan. Add the milk all at once, whisking vigorously and cooking until the mixture thickens, about 5 minutes. Add the nutmeg and salt and pepper. (For a meat or vegetable dish, my mother always added a dash of Worcestershire sauce and ground mustard, which gave the sauce some extra zip.)

MAKES 2¹/₄ CUPS

FOOD AS GIFTS

You can grow old and ugly, but if you are a good cook, the world will still beat a path to your door.
—James Beard

I love to give friends and neighbors gifts from my kitchen. Here are some that were always well received.

RECIPE_____

INGREDIENTS_____   _____

_____   _____

_____   _____

_____   _____

_____   _____

INSTRUCTIONS_____

_____

_____

_____

_____

SERVES_____ SOURCE_____

RECIPE_____

INGREDIENTS_____ _____

_____

_____

_____

_____

_____

INSTRUCTIONS_____

_____

_____

_____

_____

_____

SERVES_____ SOURCE_____

RECIPE_____

INGREDIENTS_____ _____

_____

_____

_____

_____

_____

INSTRUCTIONS_____

_____

_____

_____

_____

_____

SERVES_____ SOURCE_____

MY FAVORITE COOKBOOKS

Next to eating good dinners,
a healthy man with a benevolent turn of mind,
must like, I think, to read about them.
— William Makepeace Thackeray

Some of our favorite recipes came from cookbooks. My first cookbook was _____

_____

Other cookbooks that we used often were: _____

_____

These are some I turn to again and again:

Cookbook _____ Recipe _____ Page _____

Cookbook _____ Recipe _____ Page _____

Cookbook _____ Recipe _____ Page _____

Cookbook _____ Recipe _____ Page _____

Cookbook _____ Recipe _____ Page _____

Cookbook _____ Recipe _____ Page _____

Cookbook _____ Recipe _____ Page _____

Cookbook _____ Recipe _____ Page _____

Cookbook _____ Recipe _____ Page _____

Cookbook _____ Recipe _____ Page _____

THE PERFECT SETTING

Special china, linens, and serving accessories that I especially cherish:

China pattern _____ From _____

Number of pieces _____

China pattern _____ From _____

Number of pieces _____

China pattern _____ From _____

Number of pieces _____

China pattern _____ From _____

Number of pieces _____

My favorite linens, placemats, and napkins:

Linens _____ From _____

Number of pieces _____

Linens _____ From _____

Number of pieces _____

Linens _____ From _____

Number of pieces _____

Linens _____ From _____

Number of pieces _____

I have collected serving dishes and accessories. Some of them have stories.

Dish _____ From _____

Used for _____

Dish _____ From _____

Used for _____

Dish _____ From _____

Used for _____

Dish _____ From _____

Used for _____

Dish _____ From _____

Used for _____

Some of my favorite flower arrangements are: _____

_____

_____

_____

_____

_____

_____

_____

_____

_____

_____

_____

_____